HANDS-ON ROBOTICS

BECOMING A MEMBER OF A
ROBOTICS CLUB

MARGAUX BAUM AND THERESE M. SHEA

rosen publishing's
rosen central

New York

Published in 2018 by The Rosen Publishing Group, Inc.
29 East 21st Street, New York, NY 10010

Library of Congress Cataloging-in-Publication Data

Names: Baum, Margaux, author. | Shea, Therese, author.
Title: Becoming a member of a robotics club / Margaux Baum and Therese M. Shea.
Description: New York : Rosen Publishing, 2018. | Series: Hands-on robotics | Includes bibliographical references and index. | Audience: Grades 5–8.
Identifiers: LCCN 2017025481| ISBN 9781499438789 (library bound) | ISBN 9781499438765 (pbk.) | ISBN 9781499438772 (6 pack)
Subjects: LCSH: Robots—Design and construction—Juvenile literature. | Robotics—Juvenile literature. | School children—Societies and clubs— Juvenile literature.
Classification: LCC TJ211.2 .B375 2018 | DDC 629.8/92—dc23
LC record available at https://lccn.loc.gov/2017025481

Manufactured in China

CONTENTS

INTRODUCTION

Decades ago, robotics and robots captured humanity's imagination in film and in the pages of science fiction novels, pulp magazines, and comic books. They seemed a distant future dream. But from the factory floor to law enforcement and the military to the household, robots are now a reality. They are on the verge of becoming a huge part of many people's lives. The old image of a humanoid robot, seemingly pieced together with discarded transistor radio parts, is now a thing of the distant past. Today's robots can look like humans or animals, or take any shape or design we can conceive of.

A robot is a machine that performs actions that human beings or other living creatures can perform. At the most basic level, robots are programmed for simple actions and often repetitive ones. More advanced robots can execute more complicated tasks. Robots of the near and distant future may perform extremely complex motions and may even possess some form of artificial intelligence, and thus be able to respond to changes and make decisions much like humans do.

The robots of the future will likely come from the imaginations and hard work of those robotics enthusiasts just coming of age now—adolescents, teenagers, and college students all over the United States and around the world. In the last couple of decades, new venues for their skills have exploded in number. Robotics clubs are more plentiful than ever and are part of a growing scene of young inventors and entrepreneurs who are getting together in their spare time to build robots, some even bound for national and international competitions. It's both a fun and exciting hobby and great preparation for someone who really wants to build a career in robotics.

The technology needed to construct robots, as well as materials, parts, and tools, are more accessible and affordable than ever before. The internet revolution also makes it ever easier

The current generation of robotics clubs and teams—whether in elementary school, high school, or even college—includes the next generation of roboticists and specialists who will take robotics into the future.

for young people to teach themselves many aspects of robotics, including engineering, programming, and other disciplines. They can also connect more easily than ever with others in their hometowns or regions who share their interests. In other words, the ground has never been more fertile for starting robotics clubs than it is nowadays.

What you do in your robotics club, once you start one, is entirely up to you and your fellow club members. Whatever the case, the pastime of thinking up, designing, building, and assembling robots, and entering them in competitions, is a growing and dynamic one.

CHAPTER ONE

BUILDING ROBOTS

Although they can vary greatly in appearance, modern robots of all kinds do share common characteristics. Whether they look like the humanoid robots or take another form, most have similar component parts and operate in similar ways. A robot brain, much like a human one, acts on the moving parts, including robotic limbs, to allow the robot to perform tasks. Robots that can "make decisions," so to speak, react to changes in their environment.

First, a robot has one or more computers that act as its brain. In smaller robots, the computer is often in the form of a microcontroller, which can do even more than a microprocessor. It acts as the machine's "control": storing programs, receiving information, and sending instructions through an electrical circuit.

The circuit connects to the robot's motors (or actuators). Some robots use electric motors and electromagnets (solenoids). Others use a hydraulic system (or pressurized fluid system) or a pneumatic system (or pressurized gas system). A robot may contain different systems, too.

The motors need power to drive them. Most robots are battery powered or plug into an electrical outlet. Hydraulic robots need

From large, moving parts to the most delicate circuit boards, learning about robots and how to build and maintain them is a huge incentive to join a club where enthusiasts can develop their skills.

a pump to pressurize the hydraulic fluid, and pneumatic robots need an air compressor or compressed air tanks.

Like a human body, a robot must have parts that move. Some robots are just wheels, while others have movable metal or plastic segments. Like bones, the segments are connected with joints. The motors are the muscles that cause the segments to move when instructed by the computer and supplied with power.

Another important feature of a robot sets it apart from a regular computer. It has an ability to react to its environment. Sensors

A SHORT HISTORY OF ROBOTS

Humanoid, human-made creations built from metal or other materials that mimic human or animal actions have existed for many centuries. Automatons, or self-operating machines, have existed in many cultures, including that of the ancient Greeks. The head of the Great Library of Alexandria, Egypt, around 270 BCE, the inventor Ctesibius was one of the first to build water-powered automata.

The term "robot" was first coined in a 1920 science fiction play called *R.U.R. (Rossum's Universal Robots)*, written by the Czech playwright and writer Karel Čapek. For the following decades, robots captured the imaginations of people of all ages and were popular subjects in film, pulp magazines and comics, and novels.

A robot called UNIMATE was first deployed in an industrial setting at automaker General Motors in 1961. Robotic arms like the Rancho Arm in 1963 (developed as a tool to help the disabled) and the Tentacle Arm (developed by Marvin Minsky in 1968) soon followed. SRI International produced the first moving robot that relied on artificial intelligence in 1970. Robots would also become pivotal to the exploration of space.

In 1979, the Standford Cart robot was demonstrated negotiating a room full of chairs without human help, relying on a computer that reacts to pictures taken by the robot and estimated and reacted to distances and obstacles.

By the 2000s, computers, artificial intelligence, and robots had become incredibly advanced. Humanoid robots like the ASIMO, developed by Honda, and the QRIO, also known as the Sony Dream Robot (SDR), pushed the envelope of robotics for the commercial market, as did the mobile vacuum robot known as the Roomba, released in 2002. Other inventions, like the prototypes of Google's Driverless Car, are the first versions of products that will be available to the general public within the coming decade.

collect environmental information and send it to the computer. Sensors collect information about movement, temperature, smell, touch, sound, and light: all things that tell people how to react. Sensors may be in the form of video cameras or temperature gauges.

Team members participating in the 2010 FIRST Tech Challenge Championship examine their creation during a last check of their team's entry. FIRST is among the best-known and respected robotics contest sponsors.

SAFETY FIRST—ALWAYS

When working with robotics, as with any project involving electricity and construction tools, certain precautions should always be taken for safety.

- Check with an adult before beginning a project.
- Read directions closely before starting work.
- Work in a well-lit environment.
- Use robots only for the tasks they are meant to perform. They should not handle dangerous materials.
- Robots may move without warning when connected with their power source.
- Wear eye protection when working on or operating robots.

KITS AND PARTS

A robot is as complex as its builder wants it to be. Robot-building competitions include people as young as six years old. This shows what an accessible hobby robotics has become.

Some roboticists buy kits, such as Lego Mindstorms or kits that robot shops put together, that include nearly all the materials needed to build a robot. Common household tools such as screwdrivers and pliers may be needed as well. Kit materials can usually be used again and again.

Others enjoy picking out their own robot parts. Supplies can be found at hobby shops and online robotics suppliers. This way, they can select bigger wheels, more powerful motors, or any other specific wants and needs for their creation. A quick search of the internet can show beginners the different kinds of robots they can make. However, the

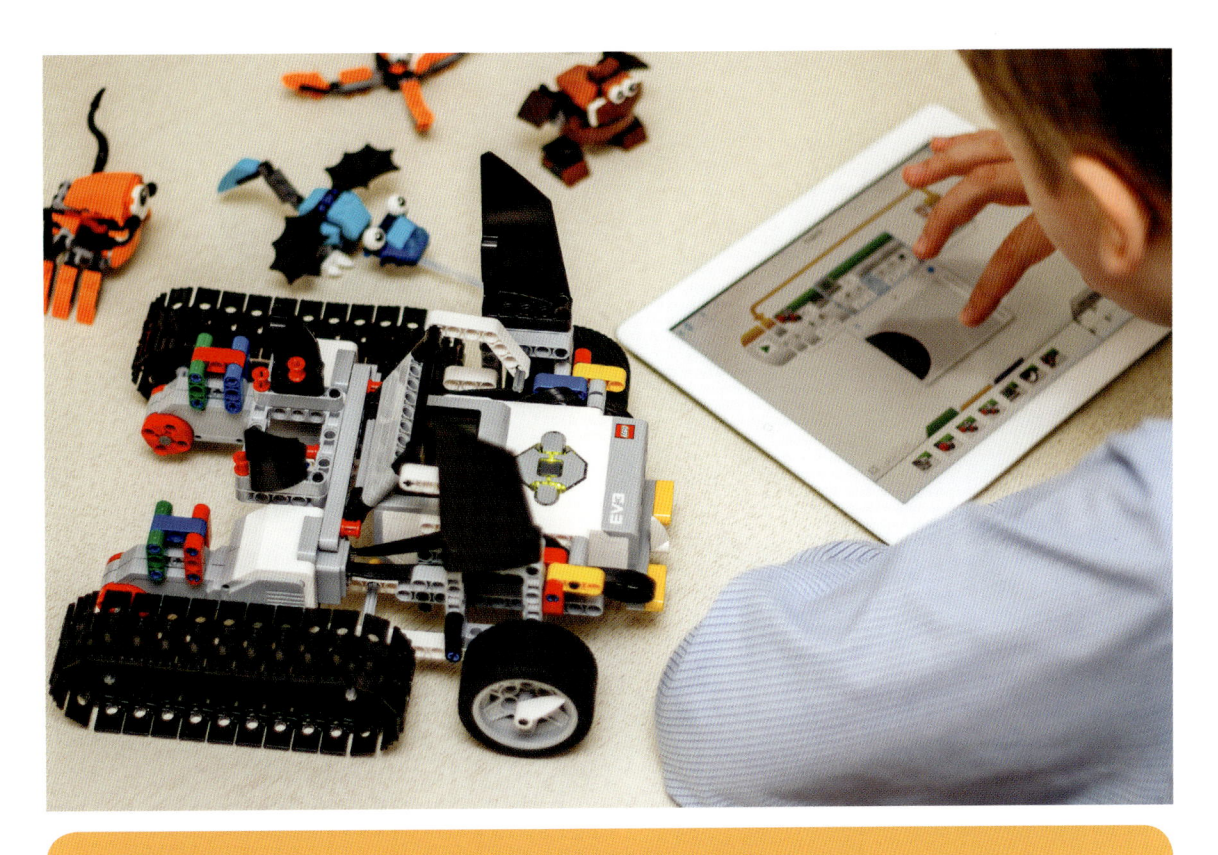

A teen enthusiast tries out commands on a Lego Mindstorms EV3 robot with an Apple iPad tablet. Commercial robotics kits like Mindstorms are great entry points for club newcomers.

simplest machines have wheels (or other movable parts), motors, rechargeable batteries, a microcontroller, and sensors. Microcontrollers and sensors come with detailed explanations of how to use and program them.

Robotics materials can be expensive, making robotics clubs even more useful for roboticists. Besides sharing knowledge and enthusiasm, people can pool robotics parts and resources. Although robotics is not a free pastime, it is an investment in the future—future robots, future fun, and future friends.

CHAPTER TWO

START A CLUB

Many people have hobbies, including young people. One's hobby might be programming, playing football or basketball, drawing comics, or bird watching. There are clubs for nearly every interest out there. With the popularity of robotics and robotics competitions, it is likely that your town, city, or region is full of like-minded fans of robotics. It is only natural that you could probably gather together some fellow students at your school or in your neighborhood and start a robotics club of your own.

Robotics clubs can be found all over the world. There are community robotics clubs, school robotics clubs, and online robotics clubs. People of all ages join these clubs, though some are meant for certain age groups. However, it is still true that many communities and schools do not have robotics clubs. Here are some tips for forming a robotics club.

MEETINGS: TIME AND PLACE

First, a robotics club needs to meet somewhere. It should be a place with enough room for an expanding club. A member's

Students who belong to the robotics club at the John D. O'Bryant School for Mathematics and Science in Boston carry their project to an auditorium demonstration as part of a ceremony celebrating new funding for STEM studies in their area.

bedroom is probably not sufficient. However, the space does not have to accommodate people building their robots. Often, robotics club meetings are for discussions. The building takes place at home, or special meetings are arranged for people to work on their projects together. Some meeting space ideas are school classrooms, library meeting rooms, coffee shops, or someone's living room or garage. All of these places require permission

Any student with a well-equipped garage or workshop can be a good candidate to host a robotics club's meetings. If the space is good enough but tools are lacking, the club members can pitch in with their own or buy what's needed.

to use the area as a meeting space. Let an adult or supervisor know how many people are expected and what materials are needed, such as chairs and tables.

A regular meeting time should be established—perhaps once a month on a certain day. For example, a meeting could take place every third Tuesday of the month at seven o'clock. This way, people know in advance when the meeting will be and can make plans to attend. Special dates can be set up for workshops or guest speakers if needed.

GROWING YOUR CLUB

So the club has a place and a time to meet. How does it get people to show up in the first place? Luckily, there are many ways to spread the word. One way is quite old-fashioned but it works—word of mouth. If a club member tells a friend or classmates, they will tell other people. If each member tells two or three people, word will really get around. Another way to let people know is by email.

There are robotics club websites on which anyone can post information about his or her robotics club. Posting on a robotics site is helpful because the people checking it are interested in robotics already. There may be similar robotics pages on social networking websites. Make sure to ask an adult about posting information on the internet. A danger of communicating openly online is that anyone can read about the club. In fact, it is a good idea if an adult is always present at club meetings.

After the club starts, it is also possible to create a website or start an online discussion group. This provides a site where information can be posted about meetings, allows people to chat about what happened at the meeting, and provides a place for members to chat about their current robotics projects. This will be a helpful trouble-shooting site for those building robots as well.

CLUB OFFICERS AND JOBS

In many clubs, people have different jobs to help shoulder the many responsibilities. The president of the club is the representative of the club to the outside world. He or she promises that the club will run a certain way to best fit the needs of the members. A secretary arranges for events and records events and ideas at meetings. A treasurer is responsible for collecting and dispensing money. When a club is first starting out, it may not need these positions. However, the larger it gets, the more responsibility should be shared. This way, there are fewer chores and tasks for each person and more time to construct and tinker with robotics.

A GOOD MEETING PLAN

What happens when people show up at a robotics club meeting? There should be a plan of action so the meeting runs smoothly— an agenda. Many clubs print out agendas so members know the plans and discussions of the club that day. It may also be wise to assign a certain amount of time to each part of the agenda. An agenda for a one-hour meeting might look like this:

1. Introductions (5 minutes)
2. Old discussions/old business (10 minutes)
3. Presentations/lectures by a group member or a special guest (15 minutes)
4. Announcements of competitions and upcoming events (5 minutes)
5. Show-and-tell/sharing of information (20 minutes)
6. Ideas for next meeting (5 minutes)

INTRODUCE YOURSELVES

Introductions are essential when the group meets for the first time. People need to get to know each other and feel that the club is a friendly environment. For the first few meetings, it would be a good idea for club members to wear name tags. After a while, people won't need name tags. However, it is always a good idea to introduce new people to the club. Perhaps one person can be in charge of "hospitality"—making people feel welcome to the club.

OLD BUSINESS

Since a club meeting only lasts a certain amount of time, sometimes topics are not fully discussed or need to be put on hold until the next meeting. Perhaps not everyone's ideas were heard. Some time should be set aside to finish up old business before new discussions. For example, imagine a club discussion

If your school provides facilities and equipment for clubs to take root, you may be able to convince a faculty member in a STEM discipline to mentor the club members and provide advice and tips after school.

focuses on a field trip the club would like to take. After the meeting, a member may hear about a new robotics museum that is opening. In the next meeting, during the "old discussions" part of the meeting, the member would have time to mention the museum.

GETTING INSTRUCTION

Part of the reason many people join robotics clubs is to learn. A valuable part of a meeting is a time of instruction. A presentation by a club member could help someone understand an aspect of his or her own projects and robots. In fact, one of the first meetings could be a presentation on how to make a simple robot.

This time in the agenda might also be used to have a special guest talk to the group. Someone who has a career in robotics can explain best how to prepare oneself for a similar career.

EVENTS AND COMPETITIONS

After people have learned about and built their own robots, they will want to show them to others. Robotics competitions

TINY ROBOT "DOCTORS"

Robotics will likely have an impact on dozens of different careers in the future. For example, microbots have far-reaching implications in medicine. The latest versions of these tiny robots are currently .78 inches (2 centimeters) long. However, in the near future, scientists hope to create robots that are much smaller, called nanorobots. Nanotechnology refers to building and manipulating amounts of matter as small as a nanometer—in other words, a billionth of a meter. Nanorobot components could be one to one hundred nanometers long or wide, with the robots themselves a good deal bigger. Still, they would theoretically be tiny enough to work easily within the human bloodstream and organ systems. They would essentially be dispatched into the human body to combat ailments such as heart disease and cancer or to help heal internal injuries or direct medication in very targeted, precise ways.

provide a great showcase. This time in the club's agenda can focus on upcoming competitions so club members can decide if they have what it takes to enter. They might also want to go as spectators. Be sure to list all event details, such as time, place, entrance fees, and transportation details.

As the robotics club grows, it may also want to hold its own competitions. First, the members can compete against each other. Then, they can challenge other clubs. If the robotics club holds a competition, there are many details to discuss, such as what kind of competition, who will judge, where it will be held, and what the prizes will be.

Members of the Eagle Robotics team, including their mentor on the right, guide a robot to deposit plastic balls at a steam pressure tank at a FIRST Robotics regional competition in Denver, Colorado.

INFORMATION SHARING

Most people join robotics clubs to see robots and show off their own. For the last part of each meeting, have a show-and-tell. Each club member can demonstrate and explain their progress on their project. After everyone is done, people can ask each other questions about their work and share information.

Some people who join the club will want to attend a few meetings before starting their own robot. Beginners may be frustrated or intimidated to show their simpler robots to people who have been building for years. Perhaps newbies can get together outside club meetings to start a project together. Put some time aside during the meeting to see if anyone has anything more they would like to share with the group. They might have a tip about a robotics equipment sale or a new website to check out.

BRAINSTORMING FOR THE NEXT MEETING

Before the meeting ends, remind everyone of the next meeting date. Mention what will happen at the next meeting, such as a guest speaker. If nothing is scheduled, ask for ideas from the members regarding new topics to cover. If meetings are run well and are helpful to builders, members will be excited to keep coming back.

MONEY MATTERS

After a few meetings, members need to decide whether to collect dues for the club. Dues are money that helps an organization in various ways. For example, if the club meetings include pizza and soda for members each month, each club member may want to pay a few dollars in dues so one person doesn't keep buying the food and drinks for everyone else each month. If the club wants to invest in special tools or equipment to share, these expenses could be covered under club dues as well. Don't forget the trophies for club competitions.

LANDING MENTORS

The most successful robotics clubs often work with mentors. It's handy to have an expert around. Robotics mentors are often engineers who volunteer to advise, teach, and encourage club members to achieve their potential. There will be times when a project seems too difficult or confusing to complete. Mentors guide the club members in developing their own solution rather than telling them what to do. Many engineering companies provide mentors for robotics clubs. Some companies even sponsor teams in competitions, which may be quite expensive.

CHAPTER THREE

THE WORLD OF ROBOT COMPETITIONS

Now the club is in full swing, and you and your fellow members are building your first robots. Once they're done, it is time to show off a bit and see how everyone's robots stack up against each other. Keep it a friendly, good-spirited competition, however. Ultimately, holding contests is a way to have fun and, most important, to improve one's skills and learn a great deal via trial and error.

There are a few basic kinds of robotics competitions. Some may be appropriate to hold within a club meeting. Others require many competing robots, so other robotics clubs should be invited to participate. An important consideration is that many major competitions require that robots be autonomous. Remote controls are often not allowed. The builder must let the robot's programming, motors, and sensors do their jobs. A well-constructed robot can move through an environment and react based on information obtained from their sensors.

TABLETOP COMPETITION

A tabletop competition is ideal for beginners. It requires a robot to travel to different areas on a field. Think of a football player

One successful FIRST club, Robotics Team 1885, known as ILITE (Inspiring Leaders in Technology and Engineering), gives a cheer during the FIRST 2010 World Championships.

running from one end zone to the other and back. Since the contest most likely takes place on a table, one part of the challenge is to make a robot that will stop without falling off one end. Each robot gets a number of chances to complete the course. There are certain time limits for each chance. If a person needs to intervene with his or her robot, that attempt may be considered "over."

Robots are usually allowed on the tabletop course one at a time. Because many robots may complete the requirements, the contest is often broken down into point values. For example, reaching one zone may award a contestant 10 points, reaching the second zone may add another 10 points, and extra points may be given for speed. Sometimes points are given out for "entertainment" value. If a contestant builds a robot that raises a victory flag, plays a song, or takes a bow, the crowd will love it.

LINE FOLLOWING CONTESTS

A basic line following competition tests a robot's ability to follow a track on a course. Robots compete for accuracy and speed. Since remote controls are not allowed, the robot must be able to follow the line using only prior programming and its sensors. In these competitions, builders decide how many sensors will help their robots "read" and complete the course in a quick and precise manner.

If a robot goes off course, a certain number of points are taken off depending on whether it can find its way back onto the course or whether its builder needs to intervene. Often each robot is allowed three chances to complete the course. The speediest time is recorded. Courses with obstacles make line following more challenging for advanced robots.

SUMO ROBOT COMPETITIONS

In sumo wrestling, a centuries-old and still popular Japanese sport, two large competitors attempt to push each other out of a circle. It takes strength, balance, and an ability to anticipate what the other person will do. Similarly, in sumo robotics competitions, two robots try to push each other outside of a circle. The first robot that touches the outside of the competition ring loses a round. The contest is best out of three rounds.

There are usually restrictions about what robots can do within the sumo ring. For example, robots can't helicopter above the ring or shoot fire at opponents. There are usually weight limitations, too, so that the contest is more difficult than a heavy robot pushing a light robot out of the ring. Instead, robots "trick" their opponents by using lights that confuse sensors, and magnets and suction to stay in place. Robots can also split into several parts once the contest starts. However, any robot part that travels outside the ring loses the round for the robot.

This robot negotiates an obstacle in the middle of a competitive event at the 2010 FIRST Robotics Competition that year called Breakaway.

Judges set a time limit for each round. They may choose to end a round if robots don't touch, become locked together, or if a time limit passes. In the event of a tie, a judge may declare the lighter robot the winner.

HUMANOIDS SQUARE OFF

Robotics competitions for more advanced builders may involve humanoid robots. Sometimes the contest is as simple as a two-legged humanoid robot walking up and down stairs. However, it is not so simple to build and program a robot that can do this. Balance is a key skill and challenge.

Another kind of humanoid competition pits the robots against each other in martial arts contests. Each robot attempts to knock out its opponent, so to speak. These kinds of contests often allow remote controls to be used since they are considered so difficult. All robots in these competitions must walk on two legs.

FIRST ROBOTICS

FIRST Robotics' various competitions are for robot builders from kindergarten to twelfth grade. FIRST stands for "For Inspiration and Recognition of Science and Technology." In 1989, FIRST was begun by Dean Kamen, inventor of the two-wheeled electric vehicle called a Segway. This organization encourages elementary and high school students to pursue careers in science, technology, and engineering. Over $12 million of scholarships are given out as prizes.

The initial FIRST Robotics Competition (for grades nine to twelve) took place in 1992 and involved twenty-eight teams in a New Hampshire high school gym. The 2010 FIRST Robotics Competition involved 1,809 teams and 45,225 students from twelve countries. FIRST Robotics Competition (FRC) robots are built from kits of parts provided to teams six weeks before the regional rounds prior to the main championship. They weigh up to 120 pounds (54 kg), excluding battery and bumpers. Also included in the kit is the description of the game for that year. The regional winners are invited to compete at the national championship.

The FIRST Tech Challenge (FTC) was also established for the high school age group. The robotics kits for this competition are more affordable than those for the other competition. First Tech challenges are different year to year as well.

For robot builders ages nine to sixteen, FIRST has a Lego League. Over 147,000 people from fifty-six different countries take part in this competition. Teams use Lego Mindstorms tech-

The FIRST Robotics regional contest for the Ann Arbor, Michigan, area in March 2010 is shown. Forty high school teams from the region competed.

nology to build their robots. Lego Mindstorms kits have Lego blocks, sensors, motors, and computer software. Lego League competitors build according to a theme. The 2010 theme was "engineering meets medicine." Robots related to ways that science helps the body repair injuries and become better and stronger. Junior Lego Leaguers tackled the topic in a different way. These competitors are as young as six years old.

A ROBOT OLYMPICS

Considering the amazing tasks that robots can be designed and programmed to perform, it is no surprise that there is a "robot Olympics." The Robot Olympiad is an offshoot of a competition called Robot World Cup. While the World Cup is a contest for college students, the Robot Olympiad is open to students of all ages. The first Olympiad took place in 1999.

Similar to the Olympics, participating countries hold National Olympiads. The winning team from each country attends the international Olympiad. It has been staged in Korea, Malaysia, Singapore, and Australia. The competition in the past has included races similar to tabletop contests, events in which robots threw objects into baskets, robot building, racecourses with ramps and obstacles, and mazes.

STEM AND BOTBALL

Botball is an educational robotics program that centers on more than just building and competition. Students use science, engineering, technology, and math (STEM), as well as writing skills in hands-on projects. The Botball year is divided into four parts that correspond with seasons. In the fall, the "Botball Research and Design Website Challenge" explores a different topic in robotics each year. Students research a question, apply a solution in a design-related task, and present their work in a website. In the winter, workshops for teachers and team leaders explore current robotics technology and how to apply it to classrooms or communities. Information and the building materials for competing robots is then distributed for the Botball tournaments in the spring.

For Botball competitions, student teams have seven to nine weeks to build their robots for the Botball regional tournament. The robots are programmed to move around a field in a fast-paced, point-scoring game without a remote control. In the summer, students, teachers, robotics fans, and professionals from around the world gather for the annual Conference on

In November 2010, the World Robot Olympiad in Pasay City, in the Metro Manila region of the Philippines, was the site of this competition between teams controlling robots playing a game of soccer.

Educational Robotics. Students and teachers exchange ideas on a range of topics. The regional champions of the Botball competitions participate in the International Botball Tournament at this conference.

A WORLD CUP FOR ROBOTS

Just as there as there is a robotic counterpart to the Olympics, there is a robotic World Cup soccer tournament. The World Cup for robots is called RoboCup. The organization behind this competition chose soccer (known as football internationally) as the main skills event because the mechanics of the sport involve many problem-solving opportunities for robot builders. The

THE THREE LAWS OF ROBOTICS

As science fiction became popular in the twentieth century, robots showed up in more books and in the pages of comic books. They took the roles of both heroes and villains. Science fiction writer Isaac Asimov downplayed the cartoonish aspects of robots and looked at them from a more scientific perspective in his work. He wrote about them as thinking machines and used the word "robotics" for the first time. In a 1942 short story called "Runaround," he listed the "Three Laws of Robotics":

1. A robot may not injure a human being, or, through inaction, allow a human being to come to harm.
2. A robot must obey the orders given it by human beings except where such orders would conflict with the First Law.
3. A robot must protect its own existence as long as such protection does not conflict with the First or Second Law.

Since 1942, many writers have adapted Asimov's laws in their plotlines. In fact, even scientists believe these famous rules are good safety measures for when robots become advanced enough to interact more closely with humans. Competitions like Botball stress that the robots have nondestructive functions, for example.

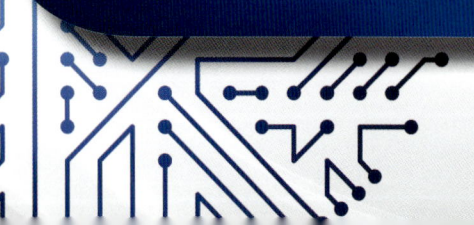

robots need to race, kick, and work together against another team. There are different "leagues." Some leagues consist of small robots, and some have robots as tall as human beings.

OTHER CONTESTS

A competition connected to RoboCup, called RoboCupRescue, focuses on constructing robots that could help with disaster rescues. RoboCup Junior is for robot builders under the age of 18, in which competitors compete in similar events, as well as robot dancing.

VEX Robotics Design System, once a supplier of parts for the FIRST Tech Challenge, now sponsors the annual VEX Robotics Competition as well as encourages instruction of robotics within classrooms.

More competitions and tournaments than those described in this book take place each year. Even if a builder is just a beginner, knowing the requirements of competitions and seeing the kinds of robots that are constructed gives an understanding of what robotics can accomplish. Similar robots can be anyone's future goal.

The kits used to build the robots are also useful to examine. Notice that in competitions such as FIRST and Botball, every team receives a similar kit of materials. However, some robots emerge victorious over others. This shows how important programming, creativity, and strategy is in winning competitions.

CHAPTER FOUR

ROLLING THUNDER: A REAL-LIFE ROBOTICS CLUB

What's more helpful than reading about how to put a robotics club together? Reading about a real robotics club in action. The robotics club of Penfield High School near Rochester, New York, is a championship competitor. Its members make up the FIRST Robotics Team 1511. They call their club "Rolling Thunder." Rolling Thunder won the FIRST Championship Rookie All-Star Award in 2004—the team's first year of existence.

Rolling Thunder members divide responsibilities and are accountable for specific tasks. Their team exhibits knowledge, skills, creativity, and hard work in every competition. The large team is divided into the following smaller teams:

- Leadership: responsible for the team calendar and activities.
- Mechanical/Construction: designs (often with the help of a computer program) and puts together the mechanical parts of the robot.
- Electrical: designs and produces electrical systems for the robot.
- Programming: creates the code that makes the robot work. CAD (computer-aided design) is a big part of creating a successful FRC robot.

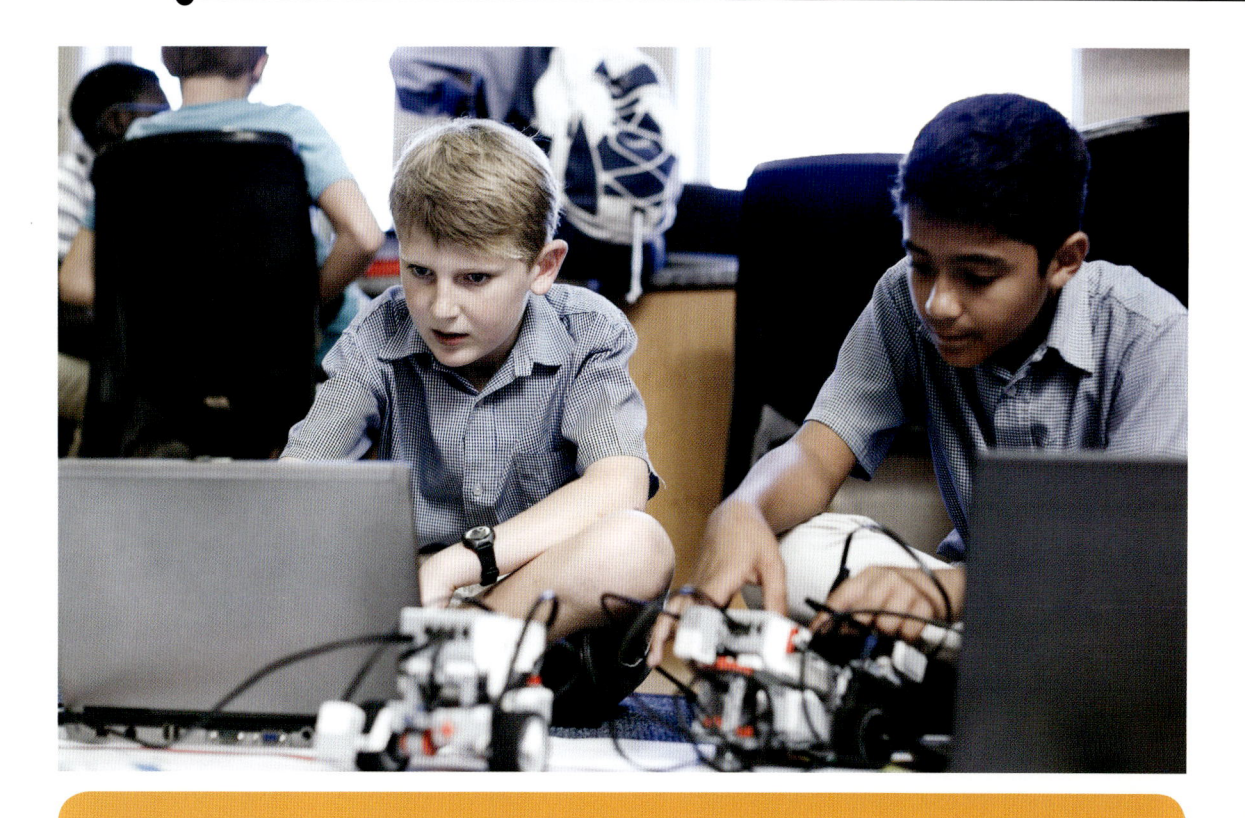

An efficient and competitive robotics club will have members who can solve problems, work together well, and complement each other's strengths.

- Finance: responsible for fund-raising and spending.
- Website: creates and maintains the website.
- Strategy/Control/Rules: controls the robot. They are also the rules experts and create strategies for the best scores.
- Spirit/Logo: creates team logos, clothing, and promotional materials.
- Animation: learns animation programs in preparation for animation competition.

On Rolling Thunder, there is room for future engineers and for those who just enjoy learning and being part of a team.

ROBOTS HAVE FEELINGS, TOO

Cynthia Breazeal, a roboticist specializing in artificial intelligence at the Massachusetts Institute of Technology, created a robot "baby" called Kismet. Kismet showed emotions through its facial expressions and movements. It had 15 computers to process information collected by its sensors. People talked to Kismet, and the robot would respond as a baby might. At one point, Cynthia thought that Kismet might need to be fixed because it wasn't reacting to its environment. The student working with Kismet was discouraged. She asked it, "Don't you like me anymore?" Then Kismet started soothing her, as if to say, "Yes, I do like you. I'm sorry."

People all over read about Cynthia Breazeal and Kismet. Hollywood director Steven Spielberg asked her to help in the making of his movie about robots, *AI: Artificial Intelligence*. Cynthia believes, in the future, robots like Kismet could be companions for people, perhaps even "grow up" and learn as people learn.

One of Breazeal's more recent projects might bring that dream closer to reality. In 2014, *Recode* reported on a newer robot she had developed, named Jibo. At a height of 11 inches (28 centimers) tall, and weighing 6 pounds (2.7 kg), Jibo, according to *Recode*, "speaks in a childlike voice, swivels its screen in the manner of a puppy's head tilt, and winks with a cartoonish eye. It can read to children, snap pictures, flag upcoming appointments, facilitate video chats and order up Chinese delivery."

Much of Breazeal's work has concentrated on making robots that act more like humans and thus put their owners and those that interact with them at ease. Beyond merely helpers on the factory floor, or mobile security cameras, robots that interact smoothly with humans will be more necessary than ever in the future. These will include caregivers for a large population of elderly citizens—in homes, care centers, and hospitals—as well as office robots that perform repetitive administrative tasks. Customer service robots that know how to be polite and friendly could also become the norm.

Many science fiction films have depicted robots inspired by real prototypes and have in turn influenced roboticists. Here, Steven Spielberg directs on the set of 2001's *Artificial Intelligence*.

GETTING PREPARED

The club members meet for the six weeks leading up to regional competitions, but they also do plenty of work year round. Rolling Thunder members complete hundreds of hours of community service, demonstrate robotics to the community, recruit new members, find financial sponsors as well as mentors, help out other teams at competitions, and even start teams and clubs in other countries. For their efforts, this club won the Chairman's Award at the 2010 FIRST regional competition in Boston, Massachusetts. The award honors the team

Robotics club members need to plan their projects and competition strategies in ways that will inform their future careers in the robotics industry.

that judges believe is a model to other teams. A very high honor, it qualified Rolling Thunder for the 2010 Championship in Atlanta, Georgia.

AIMING HIGH

The 2010 FIRST Robotics Competition challenge was called "Breakaway." Two alliances each made up of three teams compete in a match. The goal is for one alliance to score more points than the other alliance by shooting balls into the opponent's two goals. The carpeted field is divided into three sections by bumps and tunnels. At the end of the match, alliances score extra points by lifting their robot above the platform of their alliance's tower.

The match starts with a 15-second autonomous period, during which robots can use programmed code and sensors to score balls into the four goals. After the autonomous period, a 2-minute period begins in which team drivers take control of their robots and try to score balls, defend goals, and keep balls on their alliance's side of the field. In the last 20 seconds of the match, robots are allowed to expand their size and elevate themselves.

ROBOTICS CLUBS BUILD THE FUTURE

Robotics clubs build robots that do a variety of tasks. The question remains whether a complex robot can actually be "intelligent." Could it become aware of itself like the human brain makes people aware of themselves? How many computers and how much programming would it take to equal a human brain? Roboticists are not yet sure of the answers to these questions. However, robots are being built that need

Robots have been deployed in industrial production for decades. They will enter many aspects of business and leisure in the coming decades. Robotics clubs will help train the next generation of robot inventors.

less and less human intervention to complete more and more tasks.

Many of the past members of Rolling Thunder graduated high school and entered college to study engineering, computer science, and other technology-related fields. Their experiences with their robotics club gave them an invaluable head start in their education and careers. The more people start learning to build and program robots, the sooner new breakthroughs in robotics will occur. Robotics clubs provide the best classroom and real-life experiences available to young roboticists today.

GLOSSARY

alliance An association of two or more groups or individuals who agree to cooperate with one another to achieve a common goal.

animation The making of movies by filming a sequence of varying drawings to create the appearance of movement.

artificial intelligence A branch of computer science devoted to the development of computer programs that allow machines to perform functions normally requiring human intelligence.

humanoid Used to describe a being from another planet that has the appearance or characteristics of a human.

intervene To take some action or get involved in something in order to change what is happening.

logo A design used by an organization, group, or brand to represent and market themselves.

mentor An older or more experienced person who provides advice and support to younger students and enthusiasts in a particular field of interest, profession, or hobby.

microcontroller A chip that contains a central processing unit, memory for a program, memory for input and output information, a clock, and a control unit.

microprocessor The central processing unit that performs basic operations in a computer. It consists of an integrated circuit contained on a single chip.

program To insert coded operating instructions into a machine.

promotional Material created by an organization so that people will become aware of the organization.

recruit To enroll someone as a worker or member.

restriction Something that limits or controls something else.

roboticist One who designs, builds, programs, and experiments with robots.

sensor A device capable of detecting and responding to physical environmental factors such as movement, light, or heat.

software Computer programs and applications.

sponsor To provide money to a charitable cause or group for an organized event.

technology The study, development, and application of devices, machines, and techniques for manufacturing and production processes.

vacuum tube A glass tube surrounding an area from which all gases have been removed. When electricity is applied to it, a current flows through the vacuum.

FIRST Robotics Competitions
200 Bedford Street
Manchester, NH 03101
(800) 871-8326
Website: https://www.firstinspires.org
Twitter: @FIRSTweets
FIRST Robotics Competitions are among the most well known
of their kind nationwide and internationally, and their website
provides information about past challenges, upcoming contests, and scholarship opportunities.

IEEE Robotics and Automation Society
445 Hoes Lane
Piscataway, NJ 08854
(732) 562-3906
Website: http://www.ieee-ras.org
Twitter: @ieeeras
The national Robotics and Automation Society is part of the Institute of Electrical and Electronic Engineers and offers profes-
sional and student chapters.

KISS Institute for Practical Robotics
Lindsey Square, Building D, Suite 100
Norman, OK 73069
(405) 579-4609
Email: info@kipr.org
Websites: https://www.kipr.org
https://www.flickr.com/photos/botguy
KISS Institute for Practical Robotics was founded in 1994 to
make the long-term educational benefits of robotics accessi-
ble to students.

MIT Humanoid Robotics Group
545 Technology Square
Cambridge, MA 02139
(617) 253-5851
Website: http://www.ai.mit.edu/projects/humanoid-robotics-group
MIT conducts some of the most advanced research in robotics in the United States and has some of the industry's most
cutting-edge labs and collections of scholars, including the
Humanoid Robotics Group.

NASA: The Robotics Alliance Project
Public Communications Office
National Aeronautics and Space Administration (NASA)
Two Independence Square, Suite 5K39
Washington, DC 20546-0001
(650) 604-1924
Website: http://robotics.nasa.gov
Twitter: @NASA
Facebook: @NASA
NASA is the federal space agency in charge of the nation's civil-
ian space program and aeronautics and aerospace research.
It is has pioneered many advanced robots to achieve its out-
er-space exploration goals.

Ottawa Robotics Enthusiasts
Meetings at Algonquin College
1385 Woodroffe Avenue
Ottawa, ON Canada
Website: http://www.ottawarobotics.org
A group of hobby robot builders in Canada's national capital, the
Ottawa Robotics Enthusiasts meet once a month to show off
creations, share information, and work together.
Seattle Robotics Society

PO Box 1714
Duvall, WA 98019-1714
Website: http://www.seattlerobotics.org
A nonprofit enthusiasts' group whose members include amateurs
and professionals, high school students and college professors,
the Seattle Robotics Society offers newcomers to robotics online
chat sessions and help getting started with projects.

Western Canadian Robotics Society
c/o The Hangar Flight Museum
4629 McCall Way NE
Calgary, AB T2E 8A5
Canada
Website: http://www.robotgames.com
Facebook: @WCRS.YYC
The Western Canadian Robotics Society is dedicated to the
advancement of "personal robotics" and organizing robotics
competitions in Western Canada.

WEBSITES

Due to the changing nature of internet links, Rosen Publishing
has developed an online list of websites related to the subject of
this book. This site is updated regularly. Please use this link to
access the list:

http://www.rosenlinks.com/HOR/Club

FOR FURTHER READING

Asimov, Isaac, and Richard Hantula. *Science Fiction: Vision of Tomorrow?* Milwaukee, WI: Gareth Stevens Publishing, 2005.

Brasch, Nicolas. *Robots and Artificial Intelligence.* Mankato, MN: Smart Apple Media, 2011.

Chaffee, Joel, and Margaux Baum. *Engineering and Building Robots for Competition* (Hands-on Robotics). New York, NY: Rosen Publishing, 2018.

Freedman, Jeri, and Margaux Baum. *The History of Robots and Robotics* (Hands-on Robotics). New York, NY: Rosen Publishing, 2018.

Greek, Joe. *Artificial Intelligence* (Digital and Information Literacy). New York, NY: Rosen Publishing, 2018.

Hustad, Douglas. *Discover Robotics.* Minneapolis, MN: Lerner Publications, 2017.

La Bella, Laura. *The Future of Robotics* (Hands-on Robotics). New York, NY: Rosen Publishing, 2018.

Mara, Wil. *Robotics Engineers* (Cool STEAM Careers/21st Century Skills Library). Ann Arbor, MI: Cherry Lake Publishing, 2015.

Parker, Steve. *Robots in Science and Medicine.* Mankato, MN: Smart Apple Media, 2011.

Payment, Simone, and Margaux Baum. *Building a Career in Robotics* (Hands-on Robotics). New York, NY: Rosen Publishing, 2018.

Peppas, Lynn. *Robotics.* New York, NY: Crabtree Publishing, 2015.

Ryan, Peter K. *Powering Up a Career in Robotics.* (Preparing for Tomorrow's Careers). New York, NY: Rosen Publishing, 2015.

Spilsbury, Louise, and Richard Spilsbury. *Robotics.* New York, NY: Gareth Stevens Publishing, 2017.

BIBLIOGRAPHY

BBC News. "Timeline: Real Robots." September 10, 2001. http://news.bbc.co.uk/2/hi/in_depth/sci_tech/2001/artificial_intelligence/1531432.stm.

Brown, Jordan. *Robo World: The Story of Robot Designer Cynthia Breazeal*. New York: Franklin Watts, 2005.

Chibots. "Contests." Retrieved February 5, 2010. http://www.chibots.org.

Foran, Racquel. *Robotics: From Automatons to the Roomba*. Minneapolis, MN: Essential Library/Abdo Publishing, 2015.

International Robot Olympiad Committee. "International Robot Olympiad." Retrieved May 17, 2017. http://www.iroc.org.

Isom, James. "A Brief History of Robotics." Retrieved April 5, 2017. http://robotics.megagiant.com/history.html.

NASA. "The Robotics Alliance Project." Retrieved February 27, 2017. http://robotics.nasa.gov.

Penfield-Harris FIRST Robotics Team. "Team 1511: Rolling Thunder." Retrieved March 1, 2017. http://www.penfieldrobotics.com.

RoboCup. "Welcome to RoboCup." Retrieved April 2, 2017. http://www.robocup.org.

RoboRealm. "Robot Clubs." Retrieved February 2, 2010. http://www.roborealm.com/clubs/list.php.

Ryan, Peter K. *Powering Up a Career in Robotics*. (Preparing for Tomorrow's Careers). New York, NY: Rosen Publishing, 2015.

Society of Robots. "Beginners: How to Build Your First Robot Tutorial." Retrieved March 5, 2010. http://www.societyofrobots.com/robot_tutorial.shtml.

Strickland, Jonathan. "How Nanorobots Will Work." HowStuffWorks. Retrieved April 2, 2010. http://electronics.howstuffworks.com/nanorobot6.htm.

INDEX

ABOUT THE AUTHORS

Margaux Baum is a writer and editor from New York with many technology-related published credits for teens to her name.

Therese Shea is the editor and author of several educational nonfiction books. Many focus on advances in science, such as in the field of robotics. A graduate of Providence College, the author holds an MA in English education from the State University of New York at Buffalo. She lives in Buffalo, New York, with her husband, Mark.

PHOTO CREDITS